T0398091

EASTER ISLAND

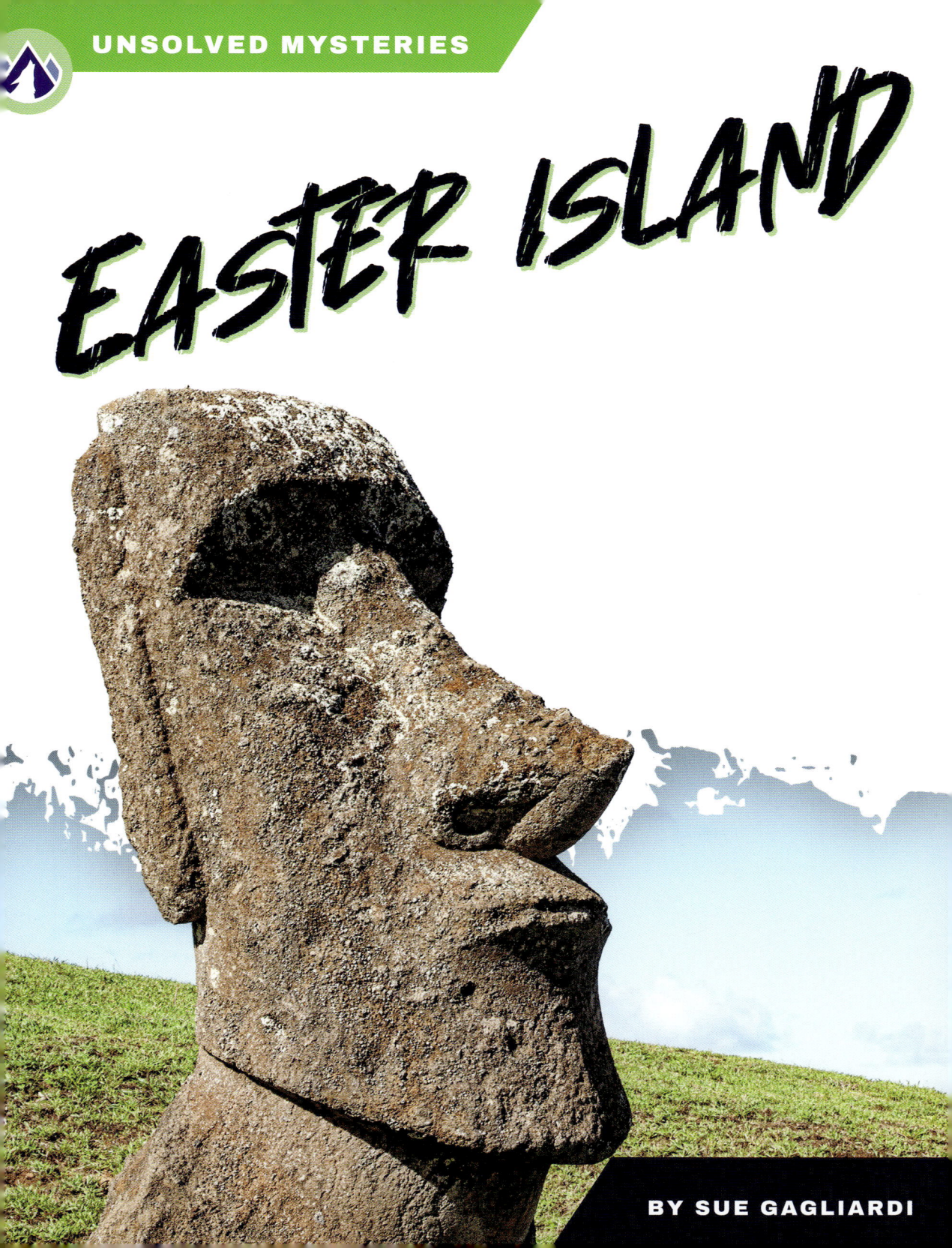

BY SUE GAGLIARDI

Apex is distributed by North Star Editions:
sales@northstareditions.com | 888-417-0195

Produced for Apex by Red Line Editorial.

Photographs ©: Shutterstock Images, cover, 4–5, 7, 8–9, 10–11, 12, 13, 14–15, 16–17, 18, 24, 26–27, 29; iStockphoto, 1, 6, 19, 20–21, 22–23

Library of Congress Control Number: 2022911838

ISBN
978-1-63738-433-6 (hardcover)
978-1-63738-460-2 (paperback)
978-1-63738-512-8 (ebook pdf)
978-1-63738-487-9 (hosted ebook)

Printed in the United States of America
Mankato, MN
012023

NOTE TO PARENTS AND EDUCATORS

Apex books are designed to build literacy skills in striving readers. Exciting, high-interest content attracts and holds readers' attention. The text is carefully leveled to allow students to achieve success quickly. Additional features, such as bolded glossary words for difficult terms, help build comprehension.

TABLE OF CONTENTS

CHAPTER 1

GIANT STATUES

Giant stone statues stand in a row. Their heads are huge. They have big noses and long chins.

Many of the statues on Easter Island are grouped together.

The statues are called moai. They can be found all over Easter Island. This small island has close to 1,000 statues. Some stand nearly 30 feet (9 m) tall.

Moai range in size. On average, they are 13 feet (4 m) tall.

People dug up some moai to study them. ▶

Some moai stand on stone platforms called ahus. Other moai lie in fields or are buried under **rubble**. All are impressive examples of stonework.

The biggest ahu has 15 moai standing on it.

KEEPING WATCH

Legends say the moai keep watch over the island. Most have their backs to the sea. They protect homes on the island. A few statues face the ocean. They welcome travelers.

CHAPTER 2

ISLAND HISTORY

Easter Island is in the Pacific Ocean. It is located to the west of Chile. Dutch explorers visited the island in 1772. They arrived on Easter Sunday. So, they called the land Easter Island.

Easter Island is more than 2,000 miles (3,200 km) west of South America.

However, native people use the name Rapa Nui. They came to the island many years earlier.

Early people on Rapa Nui lived in homes with thatched roofs.

People on Rapa Nui continue to share and celebrate their Polynesian roots.

EARLY ISLANDERS

People first came to Rapa Nui from Polynesia. They arrived between 800 and 1200. No writing from this time has been found. But some information comes from oral tradition.

Islanders built the moai sometime between 1400 and 1600. People study the statues to find out how and why.

FAST FACT

Some statues wear stone hats. Others had eyes made of coral.

The statues' hats may be topknots. They show hair tied in a ball at the top of the head.

CHAPTER 3

MYSTERY OF THE MOAI

Moai are **sacred** to people on Rapa Nui. The statues were likely made to honor chiefs or **ancestors**.

Many experts think moai were built in honor of important people who died.

Moai are made from **volcanic** rock. They were carved in a **quarry**. Some statues are still in the quarry. But many have been moved around the island.

A large crater formed on Rapa Nui when a volcano erupted long ago.

Most statues were carved from rock near a volcano called Rano Raraku.

FAST FACT

Islanders likely used stone tools to carve the moai.

Ancient islanders made many smooth roads. Even so, moving the big statues would have been difficult. One moai can weigh up to 80 tons (73 metric tons).

WALKING STATUES

Local stories say the statues walked into place. In these stories, chiefs or priests had special powers. They could make the statues move.

Many statues lie in or around the quarry. Some are tipped over or not finished.

CHAPTER 4

OTHER EXPLANATIONS

Researchers have tested several ways people could have moved the statues. In one, they put statues on wood platforms. Then they rolled the statues along a path of logs.

People often visit Rapa Nui to study or admire the statues.

24

Another method moved the statues with ropes. People used the ropes to twist and rock each statue. They moved it ahead slowly.

TESTING THEORIES

In 1982, a group of people tied ropes to a statue. Then the group split in half. Both sides took turns pulling. They made the statue wiggle forward.

Marks and grooves on the statues help people guess how they might have been moved.

Both tests worked. But people aren't sure what the original builders did. People also don't know why some statues were not moved or finished.

The fact that some statues tipped over makes experts think builders tilted them to move them.

COMPREHENSION QUESTIONS

Write your answers on a separate piece of paper.

1. Write a few sentences explaining one way the statues might have been moved.

2. Would you want to visit Easter Island? Why or why not?

3. What are the statues on Easter Island called?

    A. moai

    B. ahus

    C. Rapa Nui

4. Why would people use models instead of moving the actual statues?

    A. People don't want to break the real statues.

    B. People can't find any of the real statues.

    C. People don't study any of the real statues.

5. What does **located** mean in this book?

Easter Island is in the Pacific Ocean. It is located to the west of Chile.

    A. lost or forgotten
    B. found in a certain place
    C. moved very quickly

6. What does **arrived** mean in this book?

People first came to Rapa Nui from Polynesia. They arrived between 800 and 1200.

    A. got to a place
    B. made a mistake
    C. changed their names

Answer key on page 32.

GLOSSARY

ancestors
Family members who lived long ago.

legends
Famous stories about people, creatures, or events, often based on facts but sometimes not completely true.

models
Copies of something made for testing or practice.

oral tradition
History that is passed down through stories that are told out loud.

quarry
A pit where stone can be dug from the ground.

rubble
Broken pieces of stone.

sacred
Having close ties to a god, goddess, or religion.

volcanic
Formed from or because of a volcano.

TO LEARN MORE

BOOKS

Bowman, Chris. *Chile*. Minneapolis: Bellwether Media, 2020.

Gaertner, Meg. *Stonehenge*. Mendota Heights, MN: Apex Editions, 2022.

Hamby, Rachel. *Peru's Rainbow Mountain*. Minneapolis: Abdo Publishing, 2021.

ONLINE RESOURCES

Visit **www.apexeditions.com** to find links and resources related to this title.

ABOUT THE AUTHOR

Sue Gagliardi writes nonfiction books and magazine stories for children. She likes to explore the mysteries in our world. She lives in Pennsylvania with her husband and son.

INDEX

ANSWER KEY:
1. Answers will vary; 2. Answers will vary; 3. A; 4. A; 5. B; 6. A